Round the Houses

Round the Houses

Dan Hartigan

ROUND THE HOUSES
A SHOALS OF STARLINGS PRESS BOOK
ISBN: 978-1-913767-18-1

Text copyright © Dan Hartigan 2023
All artwork copyright © Andrew Martin 2023

The rights of Dan Hartigan to be identified as the author of this work has been asserted by Shoals of Starlings Press

All rights are reserved. No part of this book may be used or reproduced in any matter whatsoever without written permission from the author, except in the case of brief quotations embodied in critical articles or reviews.

First published in 2023

Shoals of Starlings Press logo is copyright © Andrew Martin 2020

Shoals of Starlings Press is based in Plymouth, UK

Shoals
of Starlings Press

ROUND THE HOUSES

The Gate House	9
Fort Austin Avenue	10
Stray Park	12
Upland Drive	14
Goldenbank Lodge	15
Furzehill	16
Stray Park II	17
Westbridge Cottage	18
The Crooked Spire	20
St Paul's Street	21
Wardlow Gardens	22
Grantley Gardens	23
Linketty Lane	24
Bickham Park Road	25
Oak Road	30
Ducane Walk	31
Higher Brook Lodge	32
The Providence	33
Offcuts	34
Westhill Road	36
Howard's Way	38

The Gate House

Newnham never knew how I held my breath
for you. It's easier to forget the promise than
keep it, easier to swallow truth than speak it.

I'm still crawling through your bedroom walls,
through each night, I work to right the wrongs
our fathers made, beneath the tiles we laid,

I loosen pipes, split wires like hairs with pliers
and tighten them again so water drains and
lights lighten switches you've been flicking down.

Our cold lunch and conversation are abstractions
of the stonework: clinical, precise, inflexible walls
which separate us from each other and ourselves.

But the board that falls across your heavy door
is just another lowly hurdle. A token gesture can't
prevail against this autumn's rain-fed rivers rising.

Fort Austin Avenue

Scrabble in the rain
at packs of slate that only
laugh at gloveless hands now swollen
cold. They make their weight and number known.

Hoik upon bruised
shoulders, balance not so
very carefully and rest them on the
ears that hide behind a beanie-hat head.

Aluminium-runged chore,
each step is slow and interrupted
by the poles of the implacable skeletal frame
that frustrates with its narrow hatches harrowing.

Slid across the board,
they are unstrung and taken
off to be set down with all the others
in a firing line of flatness that surrenders to the grey.

Sentimental sends you mental -
Gilbert/Gubar's loft sings noise while
Cretan balls of thick nostalgic madness
bind the memories they locked away. Either way

the felt beneath the batten's
busy breathing its dismay at being
plunged into the shadow once again, with
family albums, Christmas decorations, books.

Staples pin down the idea,
a blue-grey membranous gift wrap,
a myelin sheath that keeps the sent and unsent
letters, lost-love shoeboxes floating free from spits of rain.

There are certificates there, too;
There are musty clothes, and old CDs;
space Lego heroes made by children,
now lonely adults making children of their own;

ashtrays full of medals;
weighty desktops; token gifts;
a wedding dress worn once by Mother;
paraphernalia for dogs that died some fifteen years ago

The felt can feel each
copper nail thock-thocking
into wood and knows the truth
of slates that hide their catafalque secrets.

Stray Park

The histories of your home
are shades of golden paper.
It curls away from walls to hide
behind the radiators hung to dry.

Spider-strewn stippled ceilings hold
the surfaces of mini meringue peaks,
their artex pimples browning downward,
above delphic picture-frame ghosting.

I have turned your heartless house around,
lifted it up by four crumble-cracked corners
and broken my stumble-back, twisting the
old lead encased wires into new sockets,

stripped sun-dyed kitchen tiles away
from laughing lathe-and-plaster walls,
auctioned off accumulated nonsense,
slices of knives and loaves of dust.

The rats, in the interim, have chewed
through all that's due to go; burrowed
thrones into lofty insulation and their shit
falls through downlights and down necks.

I found one that must have died young -
its skin stretched across bones like a kite -
the bowless tail a worried sprig-like stump
I used to fling the thing into a rubble sack.

I heard you cared for both your parents,
one of them blinded by a workplace accident
and the other's early onset put life on hold.
It was a coincidental death, or so I'm told.

So you invented new ways of smoking
and remembered how to drink through
that night's inheritance. Old yourself now,
joints seizing, liver pickling, mind grinding.

I wonder how they must have found you
(in a chair, I imagine, with the telly blazing).
What stage of decay they were met with;
what purple, livid, bloated body. The rot.

I wonder what your final thought was,
on what it all hinged. I wonder where
the sparks flew as those final neurons
danced in flames of paralysis, a pyroplegia.

Upland Drive

You taught me how to swear,
and how it feels to be replaced
needlessly and against your will;
how strength amounts to nothing
amongst the rifle-fire.

The difference between Derry
and Londonderry, if there is one,
and the cruel hardness of a border
you've not seen in months and months
of Bloody Sundays.

How can the depths of a basement
be converted into a place of hope,
convalescence from alcohol addiction,
years of depression, a stepson's cancer
hiding in his head?

The waters are still, cold and bottomless
but there are sixty cubic feet of concrete
around the northern side of your pool,
built from stones you held in both hands,
in both his pockets.

The promises feed tenacity, yet here lies
the mindset that kept telling you to rise
from a second marriage, or a broken back.
Sixteen pins and a partly-severed cord
kick your feet out.

Goldenbank Lodge

Before I got there, the hallway that separates your house
from your mother and your quiet single-parent son
was one smokey end of a snooker room.

Before I got there, your mother's annexed flat-pack kitchen
was a private, heated, indoor swimming pool
and your drains were still blocked.

Before I left, I heard your mum turning her car over;
the sound of table tennis outside your office;
undiluted hypochlorite sloshing.

As I left the moss was being scorched by the invisible fire.
The woodlice and spiders ran for lives ending in panic,
the air around them making my eyes water.

Afterwards, I heard it rain and the chemicals drained,
purging all life from the roof tiles and brickwork
of your now immaculate driveway.

Furzehill

Born in a box, he'll die in a box:
tails can't wag a locked cage loose.
His eyes won't water the news
and the smell of his mess will fade
over time.

But as we lift the hardboard floor,
crinkled by damp and urination,
and lean it against the rosettes
and certificates of affixes, we can
see your end.

Nailed to a wall are pastel portraits
of your prizewinning predecessors -
Irish, smooth foxes and Scottish
are caught and framed and hung there
before you.

Old Coco the whippet's his favourite.
Her days are numbered, weightless,
skittering over the new porcelain tiles,
her pale bones pushing from under
a skin-thin veil.

The barking and whimpering halts
between the flies and the rainstorm
between the smooth long planes.
We rub it in and wipe down the grout
to keep you out.

Stray Park II

I feel like writing, digging, but it's been done.
Somebody always gets there, prematurely.

The mattock curls away the soft putty earth.
I flick through the hardcore, unearth worms.

But Heaney isn't here now, he's under the cut slab
and the level sand, the footings for each step.

I'm delving down to sketch a passing madness,
my visions reified in this new sequence of blocks.

Concatenations of squares make me stiff as
I'm forced to my knees. Check my straightness.

Napes of necks redden in their admiration. Falling
from grace as I finish, I feel myself rising again.

Westbridge Cottage

There's a history to sixty four
whitewash cottages which,
although a square number,
have walls that are as level
as an 1850s pyramid scheme.
We gave one's bathroom some
new right angles, a good clean,
and the very first family of ten
enjoy it in my waking dreams:
a copper man with none to rub
together but his pyrite hands,
his hair and teeth are all green
from the patina of paying it
forever forward to Francis,
but Bedford barely blinks.

As the recent past is cleared
I catch sight of new money:
a single sticky Japanese yen
had fallen down between pan
and toilet roll holder. I told her
that the change was all the
same to me, nouveau riche,
just as good as all the rest.
As word play flies overhead,
I felt sure that even the
galvanised ghosts of miners
would have appreciated the
paradox - wry smiles might
have wrung from misfortune.

Kintsugi cracks catch at bags
I'm hauling to the tip, dragging
into skips like scraps of paper
down Winston's memory hole.
The yen, men, copper stopper,
clean dreams, blinking, stinking,
all into the bags they're swept,
discarded all. Nothing left
to recall their cloistered histories
just blossoms, on a wet, black sea.

The Crooked Spire

We put in a steel to set straight
the sagging ceiling and destroy
the fuschia toilet walls, painted
to signify a cisgender; a proclivity
for a sit-down wee; and made up
make-up conversations.

Acrow props and second-hand
scaffold planks are repurposed
to stop the roof from caving in.
Jack posts and jackhammers
start automatically at the top,
and go down on you who are:

someone else's lurid femininity.
Identity is more subtle than colour.
See-through condensate running
down tiled cheeks screams your
name louder than amaranthine
ever could.

We left the soil stack hanging there:
a grotesque and oily coat-stand tree,
the redecoration and refurbishment
of which I'll never see, but I hope
for more neutrality to be sung by
softer shades of grey.

St Paul's Street

The basin waste was wrapped
in a putty clay fist squeezing her
swan's neck. I peeled fingers
away to clean the swollen trap
that sang of hairdye, nails, spit
and closer shaves with things he
never intended for the plug hole.
I replaced what had worn down
with stronger stuff. I picked up
pieces of myself from the floor
leaving sealant curing with time
enough for a milky cup of tea.
Apologetic texts next day say
that despite best efforts, she
still weeps after each use.

Wardlow Gardens

The fence peeled away
like a chocolate wrapper
around melting brambles
to reveal the neatest pink
artichoke of a rosehead
that pushed towards the light,
a swimmer treading water.

We pulled rotten posts up
and lifted the line away;
we dragged out rubbish
piled along the border,
stopping neighbours' dogs
from scratching through
and marking their territory.

The single scoop of petals
neglected by nextdoor
ultimately go nowhere.
We replaced the panels,
threw it into shade as deep
as the earth my first love
dug its fibrous roots into.

Grantley Gardens

Tempered glass has a weight to it
that could come down and split worlds.

Double-glazed, but not sound proof
when it thunks cement and splinters fly.

The snails running along one side
are brown tears streaking down the pane.

Watercolour morning glories watch
from frames behind frames, glass over glass

The room ages immediately while
paper, photos, carpets all go up in oxygen.

Linketty Lane

Nothing much depends on
a wheelbarrow of concrete
to fill the four cubic metres
of an extension's foundation.

One hundred and sixty
bags of ballast beating
around the drum, mixing
ratios with water and noise.

The sun-squeezed sweat
pours just as easily. Skin
roars red as the mixer while
seagulls scream their truth

above a girl with her rucksack
waiting for friends to take her
from the jumbled bungalow
and into a less crowded life

where parents are present,
not wrestling with addiction;
where beds are not sofas
and bookshelves not tables.

Bickham Park Road

1.

Floorboard tabloids and broadsheets
revealed by foam-backed carpets,
show Blair's smile had lost its shine
and Bill Murray could do no right.

AOL was busily replacing top shelves,
people still sold houses and themselves,
and columns of god knows what else.
Lines made of made-up lines laid over lines.

Eugene Guillevic is dead, I read;
reached the end of his parallels
and wrestled the socialist party
into the grave, looking for Cézanne.

Obituaries turn to "Fake Breasts and Fargo".
"All the Fun of the Pharaohs" is advertised
beside a biting critique by Anthony Thwaite
of how Heaney and Hughes might collaborate.

"Everyone's Blood" is beneath my feet
in headlines, there's "No Place on the Board"
for rebel Saudis, or white mercenary terror,
"Cromwell's Men are Moving in Nextdoor".

A "Boy who Dared to Live" shares space
with a "Father's Tribute to [a] Son he Loved".
Paper pulses, and drafts spool from outside
windows, sliding between slats of unrefined pine.

2.

I have cut out your heart
and stacked it to one side
in neat little criss-cross piles.

The dust from the incision
got in my hair and clothes
and made my eyes rusty.

The bricks had been used
to fill cavity walls another left
between the two houses.

There are lead pipes where
veins should be, aortic chimneys
and blown plaster platelets.

Your heart hits the floor
as an iambic mess of red clay,
each piece walking a plank.

Crumbs of it bounce and roll
until they're lost between joists
shielding us from the void.

3.

Boldness becomes you:
a flick switch in the dark,
tethered to the silent rot,
screwed into skeletons.

a service bell beyond.
I reach into the rafters
that groan like gargoyles,
stroke the smooth dull dome,

carefully bring it home from
its century of fitful sleep,
and clean it in the knowledge
that the price to shine is steep.

4.

Wires frayed,
worked loose
from the chinks
in your mansion.
Feeling in darkness
for the missing link.
Light-bringer!

Fuses blown,
mind blown,
fingers licked
and locked
boney tongues.
Faster than electric,
quick as the dead.

Eyes roll upwards
and melt away.
Nerves on fire,
a world on fire,
teeth ground down
to powdery chalk.
Plastic petrichor.

A hairline fracture
breaks its way
through columns
where life was.
The void inflates
like a negative reel
of The Big Bang.

5.

It's a curious phrase
that falls from the lip
in puckered distaste
like a rotten rose hip.

We're letting you go.

Were we all embraces?
Did I tie my fate to you
and hang in suspense?
Was the tension moved?

We're letting you go.

You have no idea
which way is up.
It suits me just fine,
I've had quite enough

We're letting you go.

I dust off my knees,
I throw on my coat,
I swallow my joy,
I grab at my throat.

Oak Road

You give life away
piecemeal, like
inches of land
from a boundary
lined by wobbling,
rollover palisades
posted into weak
knees. Your loose
joints rusty spurs,
rain makes them
swell, panels groan
against each other.
You endure
comfortless nights
where youthful feet
cut corners where
you used to draw
lines out of wood;
cut closer to you,
cutting deadweight,
cutting dreamy deals
in shrink wrap sleep
shrinking, sleeping
your world away.
Gravel boards
shuffle forwards
when you wake,
until they wake
you one morning,
knocking gently
at your door.

Ducane Walk

He went to sea on a beautiful
Christmas Eve leaving his wife
and children behind to suffer
the noise and destruction of
their gable end extension.

And there was no annoyance at
his untimely deployment, only
a stoic shrug, acceptance that
this will keep us warm and fed,
will keep us all awake in bed.

Their floor arrived string-wrapped
on the back of a Jewson's sleigh.
I posted it through their window
and laughed heartily to the tune
of World at One and six mince pies.

It was painted, decorated, fitted,
and insulated. I got stuck digging
their soakaway on my way out,
leaving steel-toecapped footprints
that morning rain would melt away.

Higher Brook Lodge

It's concrete over concrete
we spent the day taking away.

Layer upon layer, demoralised
ground-bouncers, hands shaking.

Shovelling up our hearts
and hunger into bags -

rubble sacks dripping with
weight from our shoulders -

Tonnes of hardcore left by layby
not enough to break our backs.

Birdsong murdered by our noise,
gentle breezes, trembled trees.

Not enough, or too much. These
lightning cracks are dragon's teeth.

The Providence

Here's to the slow burn of a fire
and the soft snores of a dog soothed to sleep
by the words of this ragtag rabble.

Here's to the hats and coats, the scarves and suits,
the diamond skulls and upturned glasses.

Here's to the sound that time makes as it passes,
through crowds it rouses with quart-hourly chimes.

Here's to eulogies, and heresies, of glassy orbs
that hang like swords of Damacles, above each poet
rising from the rubble of their rhymes.

Between butler frogs and soapstone elephant gods,
it's these patient effigies that hear me most.

See all sunswept paths of wallpaper coasts
never walked, not yet walked, I will walk.

Here's to the listening, here's to the talk.
Here's to all of us, to the lifting of feet
after miles of planting them out on the street.

There's no joy in the work but for those born to do it,
but we're all born to do it, yes, we're all born to do it.

So here's to the work, and the joy and the rest.
Here's to the Courage, and here's to the Best.

Offcuts

1.

I broke its neck swinging.
Cut away at Earth spinning
horizontally, supine,
like a scythe undermining
the footing of a garden wall.
Watch your feet, watch it fall.

2.

builder's tea
liquidity
often free
restores me

drop of milk
smooth as silk
no sugar
time took her

3.

to worry about
one less thing
is
looking for me
when I'm gone

4.

Lights in a box,
ships in a bottle,
rain in pockets.

Tools in a box,
beer in a bottle,
raining buckets.

Fools in a cage,
heaven on-stage,
prompter says "fuck it".

5.

It's this way up
I kept telling you
and you mutter that
the box is heavy
even though
we carry it
– the day's toil –
to bury our grief
with both feet in
a box of tools
we're shouldering
someone's demise
up this way... it's

Westhill Road

As I go round all the houses,
like the clouds go round the houses
and the roads go round the houses
and the fences round the houses
and the scaffolds go round houses
and the tiles drape round the houses
and the gutters hang round houses
and the downpipes go down houses
and the render goes round houses
and the rust goes round the houses
and the pipes go round the houses
and the wires go round the houses
and the light goes round the houses
and the steps step round the houses
and the doors slam round the houses,
all these chores I've found in houses.

Lost and found abound in houses:
so much clutter round these houses,
litter lies about these houses
like life lies around these houses.
Sparrows nest inside these houses,
like to rest around these houses,
hope for warmth about these houses.
Rats run rings around these houses;
skulking jackals surround houses
digging in around these houses
and the darkness found in houses.

Even houses go round houses...

Houses go round nurseries,
baby blue, or pink, or grey,
houses choke the rats and mice,
keep cold and damp away.
Houses keep their business shelved,
stow their keepsakes in the loft,
houses round your life, your self,
keeping safe behind the lock.

And houses wrap round lightning wires,
and houses play with pipes and fires,
the houses wrestle with their rust,
and rend their render all to dust.

Yes they flay themselves down to the redbrick.
They peel away blistered paint and damp scabs
and settle when they're told they shouldn't settle,
and their timbers twist or softened crumble under
feeble furtive fingers all at least a tenth their age.

And their gutters sag and downpipes clog,
and their tiles are whisked away by God,
and the fences lean and scaffolds crowd
round houses building houses in the clouds.

Howard's Way

It's a fairly straight road
that runs from A to B,
especially when broken down
into bite-sized, tarmac chunks.

And it's a fairly straight path
that leads to the door of your
sometime house... Sometimes
though, we wish for obstacles.

And it's a straight hallway
from the door to the kitchen.
Soon-to-be-gone laminate
boards itching green in the sun.

Each board is a straight line.
The joints between them though,
are unparalleled. Such a single
minded, one-dimensional grift:

a unilateral con. I examine each
tongue and groove and it's gone.
You could step on each one now,
but now they're gone. Look at us.

We thought we were together
and perhaps we were for a while
held together by an interpersonal
vacuum, slowly dying in the sun.

It's a straight line that connects
A to B, it's a straight lace threading
its way through jacket sleeves.
It's a one-sided die that troubles me.

Dan Hartigan is a poet. A plumber from
Plymouth. A parent. A part-time teacher.
A person. Struggles to understand
pineapple. Never been to Poland.
Other things beginning with P.

www.ingramcontent.com/pod-product-compliance
Lightning Source LLC
Chambersburg PA
CBHW031943070426
42450CB00006BA/873